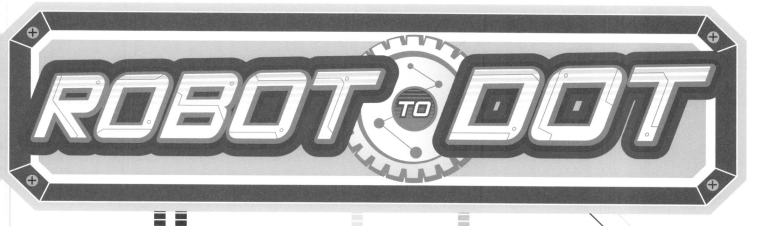

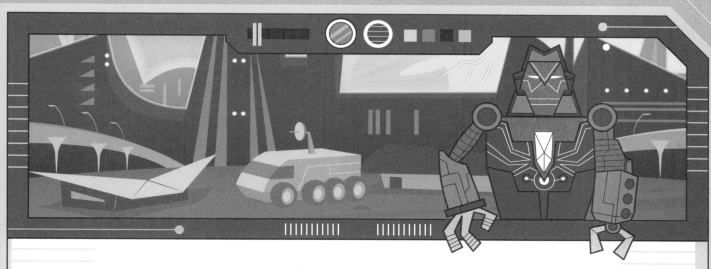

Published in 2016 by: Spirit Marketing, LLC
700 Broadway Boulevard, Suite 101, Kansas City, MO 64105
Visit us at hellospiritmarketing.com
© 2016 Spirit Marketing

ISBN: 978-0-9965998-8-7

Designed in Kansas City by Chris Evans,
Patrick Sullivan, Matt Loehrer, Jason Bays, and Chris Simmons.

For information about custom editions, special sales, and premium and corporate purchases, please contact Spirit Marketing at info@hellospiritmail.com or 1.888.288.3972.

Printed 5/16 in China

ROBOT REPLICA

CAN YOU FIND THIS BOT'S EXACT MATCH FROM THE BOTS BELOW?

GIVE YOUR ROBOTS NAMES

BOT 1

BOT 2

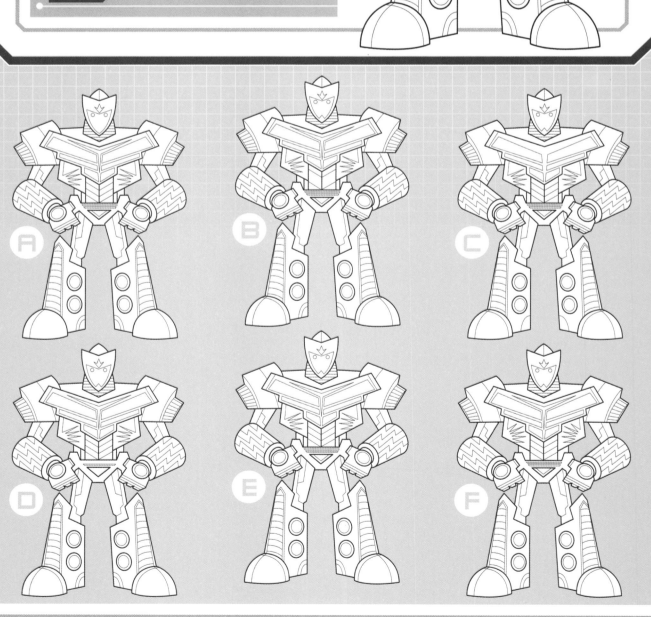

A   B   C

D   E   F

DRAW-A-DROID

FOLLOW ALONG WITH THE STEPS TO DESIGN YOUR DROID.

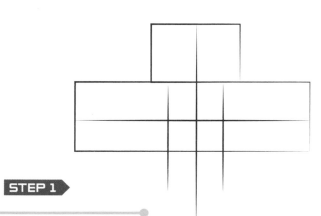

STEP 1

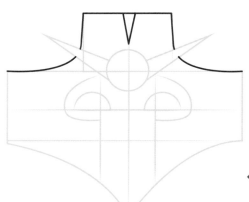

STEP 4

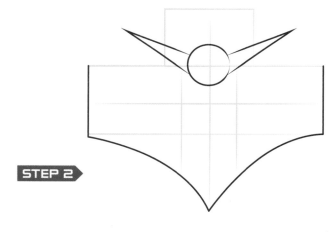

STEP 2

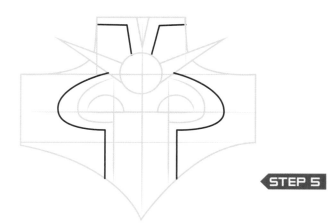

STEP 5

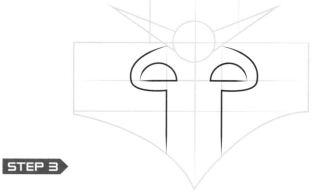

STEP 3

STEP 6

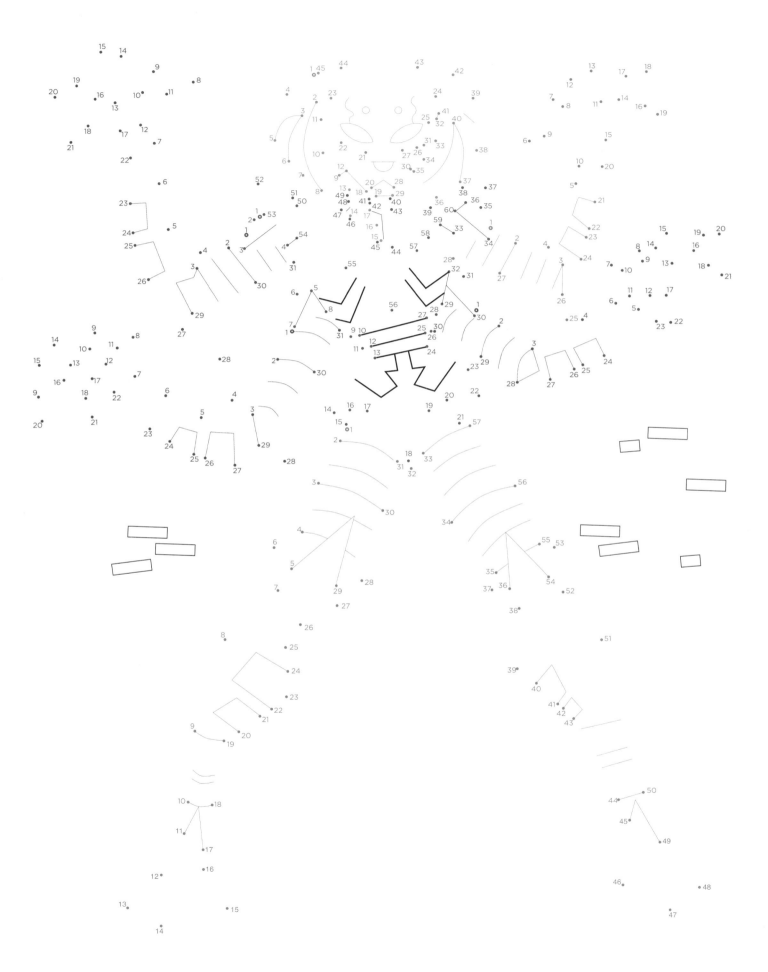

NAME YOUR ROBOT:

FACTOIDS & FUNNIES

- The word "robot" comes from an old church Slavic word "rabota", which means "servitude of forced labor".

- One of the first robots appeared in the play "Rossum's Universal Robots" (1920).

- Currently, there are more than 1 million industrial robots being used for jobs, and more than half of them are in South Korea.

- The first drawings of robots date back to 1495, with Leonardo da Vinci's plans for an armored humanoid machine. A robotist name Mark Rosheim helped create a smaller version for NASA to use on Mars.

- Mars robots, named Spirit and Opportunity, were built to last 90 days. Spirit lasted six years and Opportunity just rolled into its 12th anniversary on Mars!

- The world's first humanoid robot, named Elektro, made its debut in 1939. Elektro was a seven-foot-tall walking machine, that could speak more than 700 words!

FUNNIES

Q WHAT IS A ROBOT'S FAVORITE TYPE OF MUSIC?
A Heavy Metal!

Q WHAT WAS THE ROBOT'S FAVORITE NURSERY RHYME?
A Ro, Ro, Ro your bot, gently down the stream...

Q WHAT IS A ROBOT'S FAVORITE SNACK?
A Computer Chips!

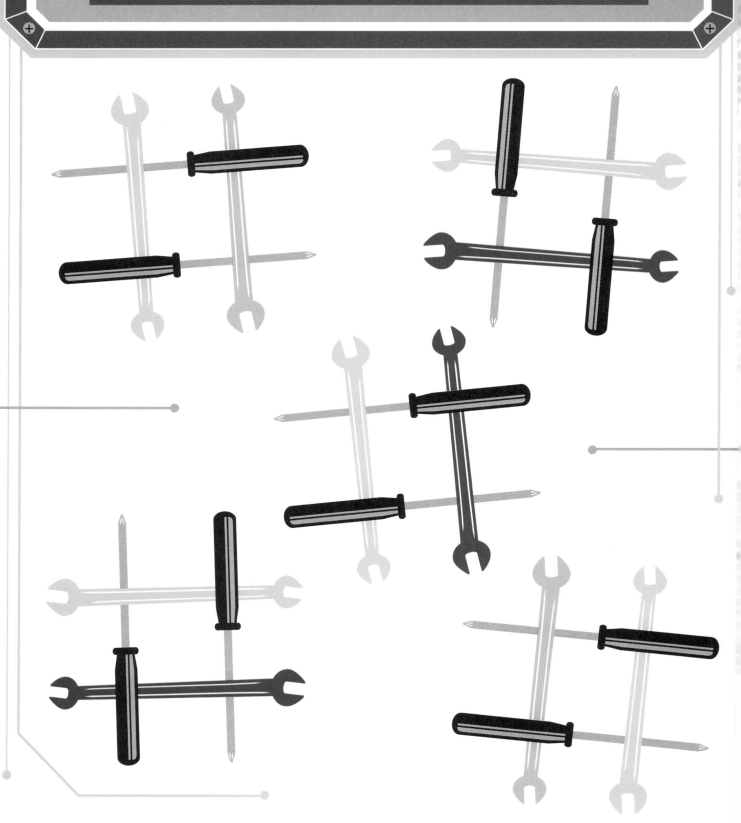

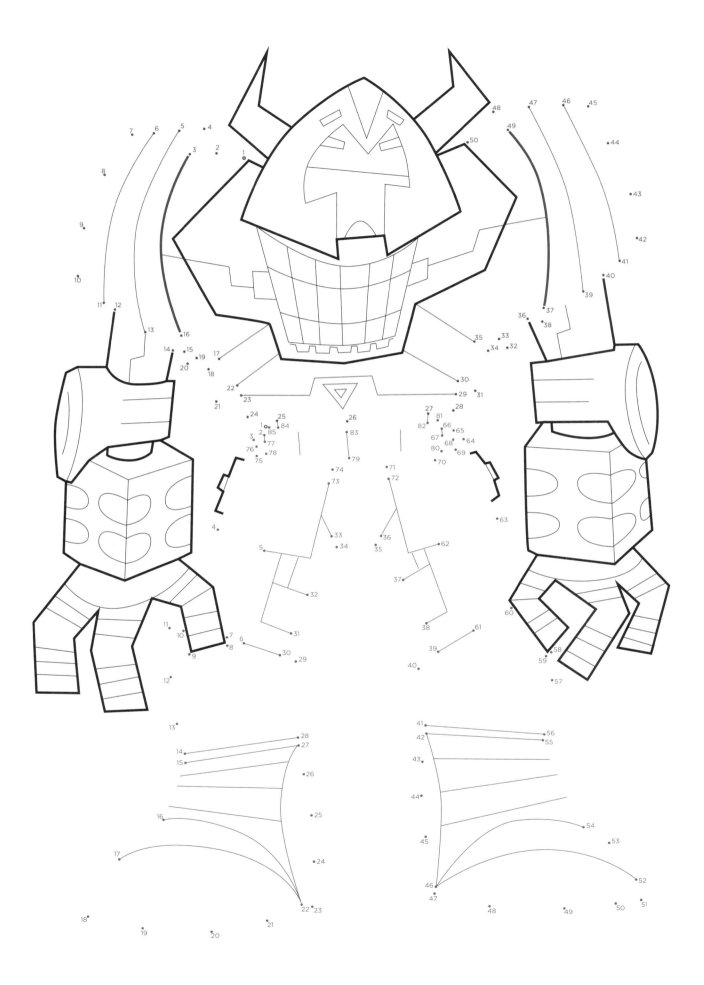

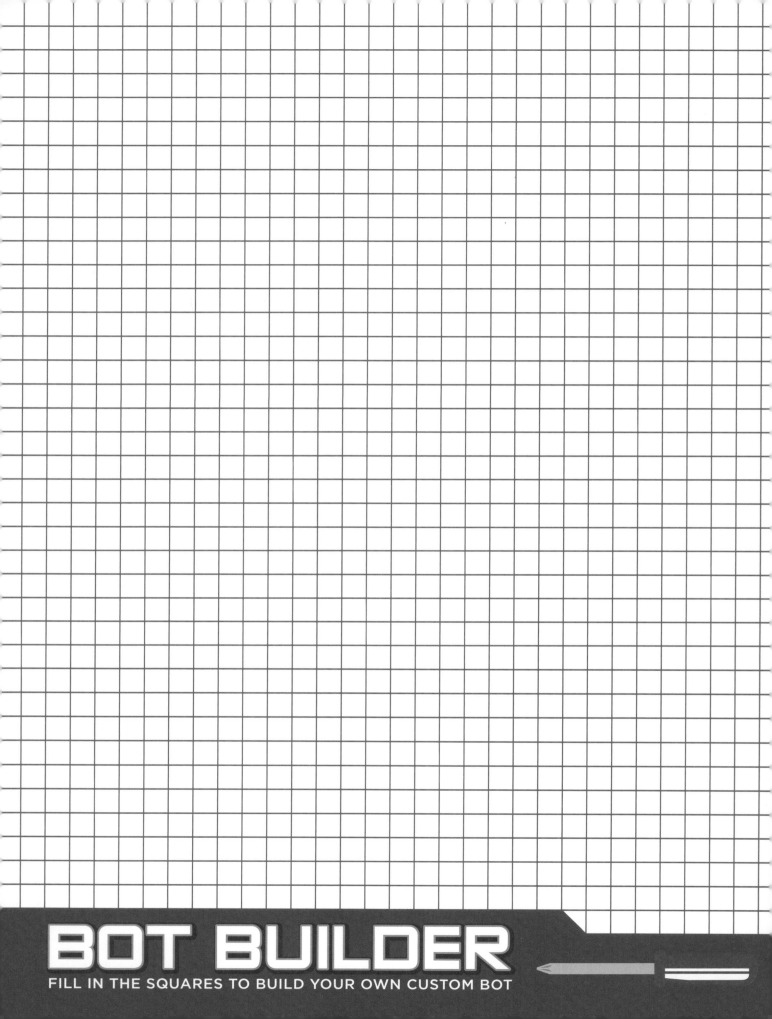

```
B C O M P U T E R P U R X T J I V
E D H C O N L Q S K B A T T E R Y
A G M F S C R E D H O R E D E B B
C K A D E N A P C M L A S E R M G
O Q O F N W S B F G T S A B K U D
N Y E A S R E D H C S K W Y Z R A
N T O H O N R O C K E T S T E N E
E G U T R R B C S O H E X R L R O
C D W M C S G W H E E L S S E S S
T A I F G B F G I A G Q S K C B M
O E R S M K W Y Z N A G M F T K O
R O E A M O T O R C G A M C R Y N
S Q S D H E W S B K U S B G O T I
R E D E B B M S A G E A R S N D T
B C S O H E M O E D H C O N I S O
S C A B L E S F R K R U D B C B R
G R I V E T S G M Y X T J I S A O
```

☑ COMPUTER   ☑ MEMORY   ☐ WIRES   ☐ LASER
☑ CONNECTORS ☐ MOTOR   ☐ ELECTRONICS ☐ ROCKETS
☑ BOLTS   ☐ WHEELS   ☐ GEARS   ☐ RIVETS
☑ BATTERY   ☐ CABLES   ☐ SENSOR   ☐ MONITOR

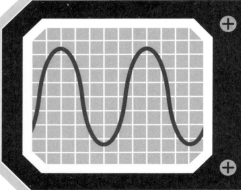

ROBO-WORD SEARCH

INSTRUCTIONS: FIND ALL THE ROBO-WORDS.
THEY MAY BE HORIZONTALLY, VERTICALLY OR
DIAGONALLY PLACED. END OF TRANSMISSION.

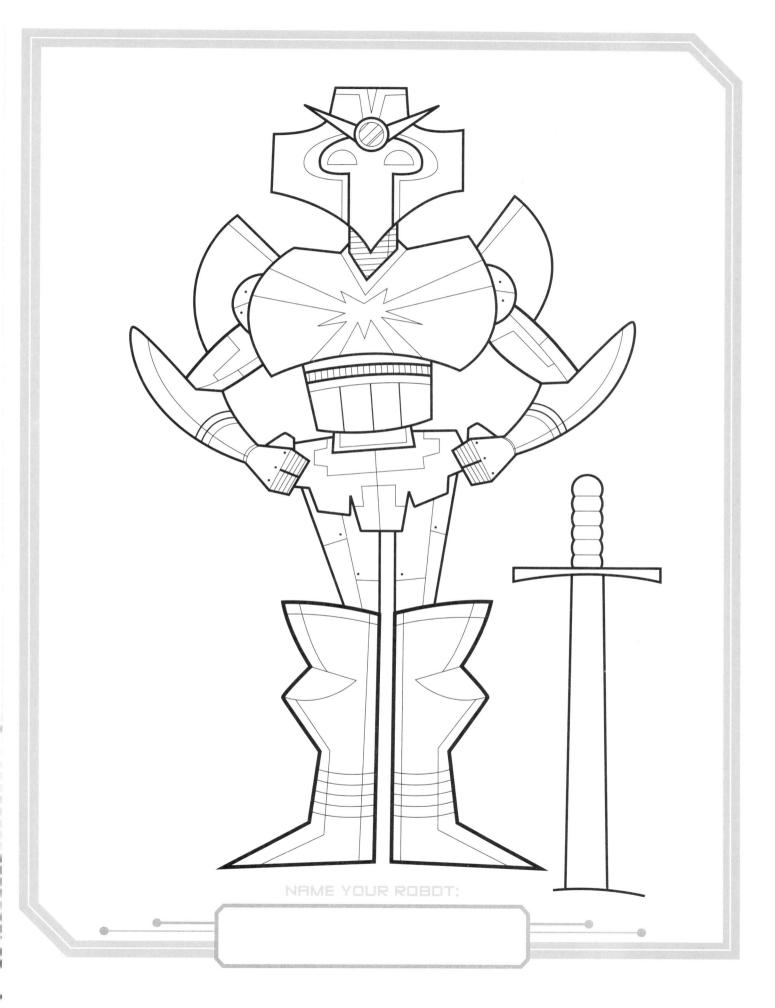

NAME YOUR ROBOT:

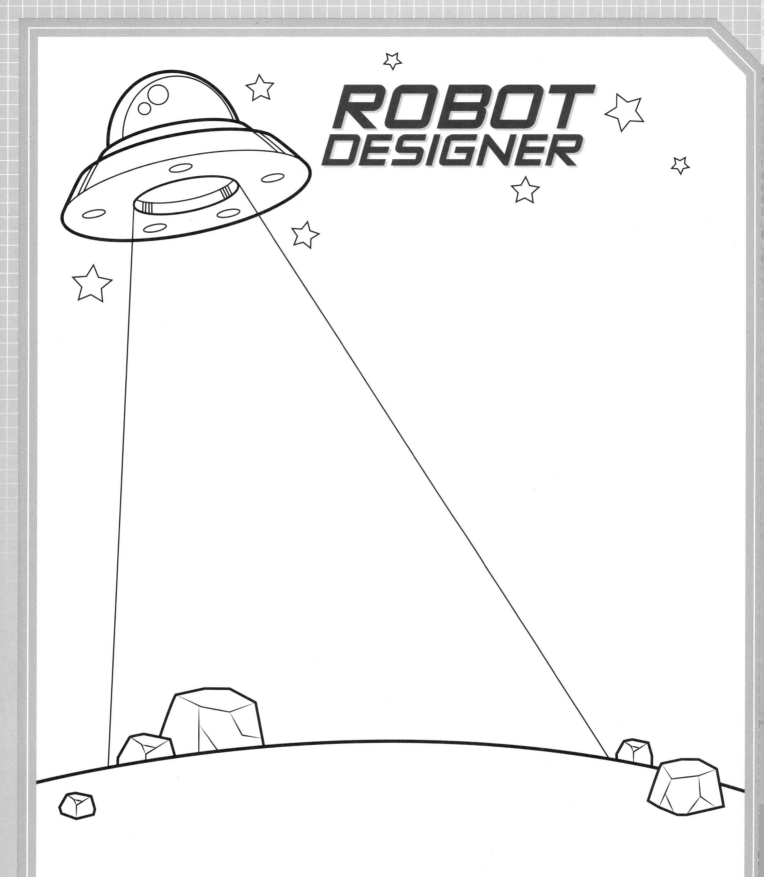

ROBOT DESIGNER

CREATE YOUR OWN CUSTOM ROBOT HERE
(YOU CAN DRAW OR USE THE STICKERS FROM BACK OF THIS BOOK)

ROBO-MAZE MADNESS

FIND YOUR WAY THROUGH
THE DIGITAL MAZE FROM
START TO FINISH!

START

FINISH

DRAW-A-DROID

FOLLOW ALONG WITH THE STEPS TO DESIGN YOUR DROID.

STEP 1

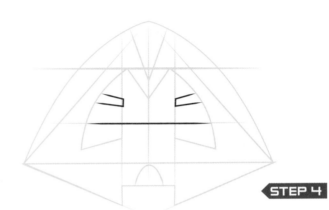

STEP 4

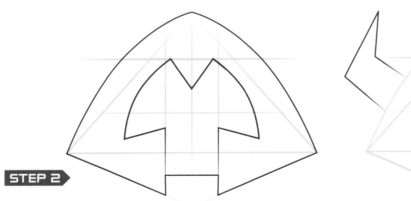

STEP 2

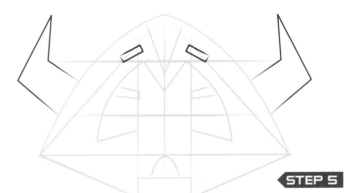

STEP 5

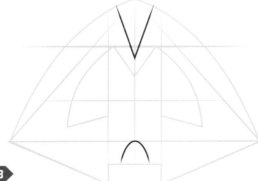

STEP 3

STEP 6

BOT BOXES

YOU'LL NEED TWO PLAYERS. TAKE TURNS CONNECTING THE DOTS. WHEN YOU COMPLETE A BOX, PLACE YOUR INITIALS IN IT AND TAKE ANOTHER TURN. KEEP TAKING TURNS UNTIL THERE ARE NO MOVES LEFT. THE PLAYER WITH THE MOST BOXES WINS THE GAME.

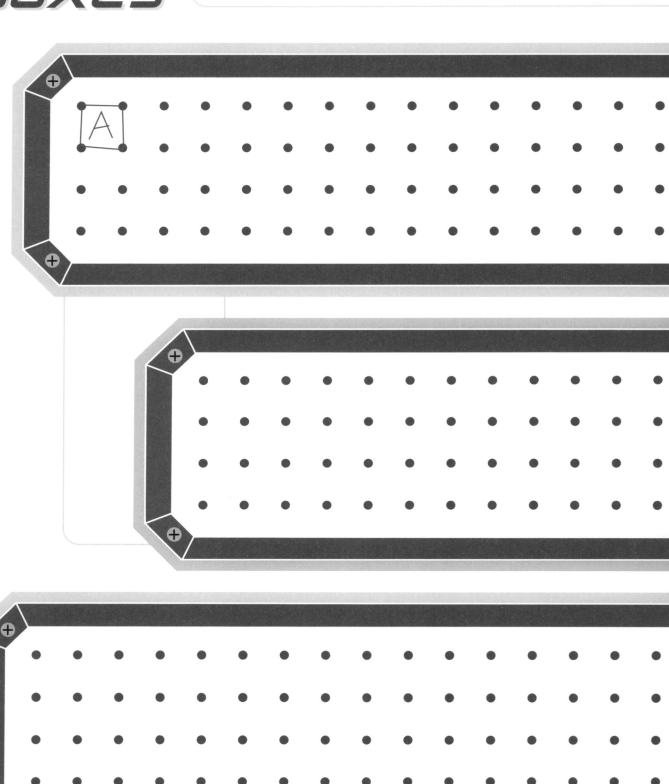

NAME YOUR ROBOT:

ROBOT
DESIGNER

CREATE YOUR OWN CUSTOM ROBOT HERE
(YOU CAN DRAW OR USE THE STICKERS FROM BACK OF THIS BOOK)

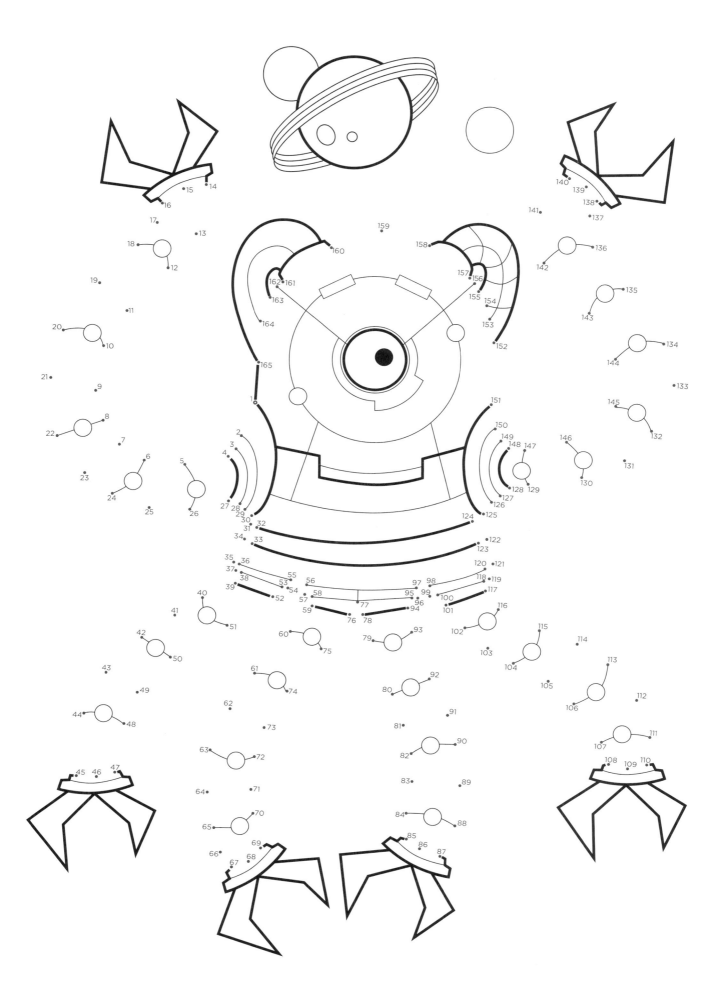

MEGA MATH

USE THE VALUES OF THE ROBOT SYMBOLS
BELOW TO SOLVE THE MATH PROBLEMS

 =1 =2 =3 ⚡=4 =5 =6

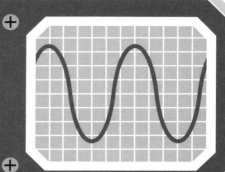

ONE   + + + ⚡ = [ ]

TWO   + − + = [ ]

THREE   + ⚡ − ⚡ + = [ ]

FOUR   + − + = [ ]

FIVE   − − ⚡ + = [ ]

SIX   ⚡ + − − = [ ]

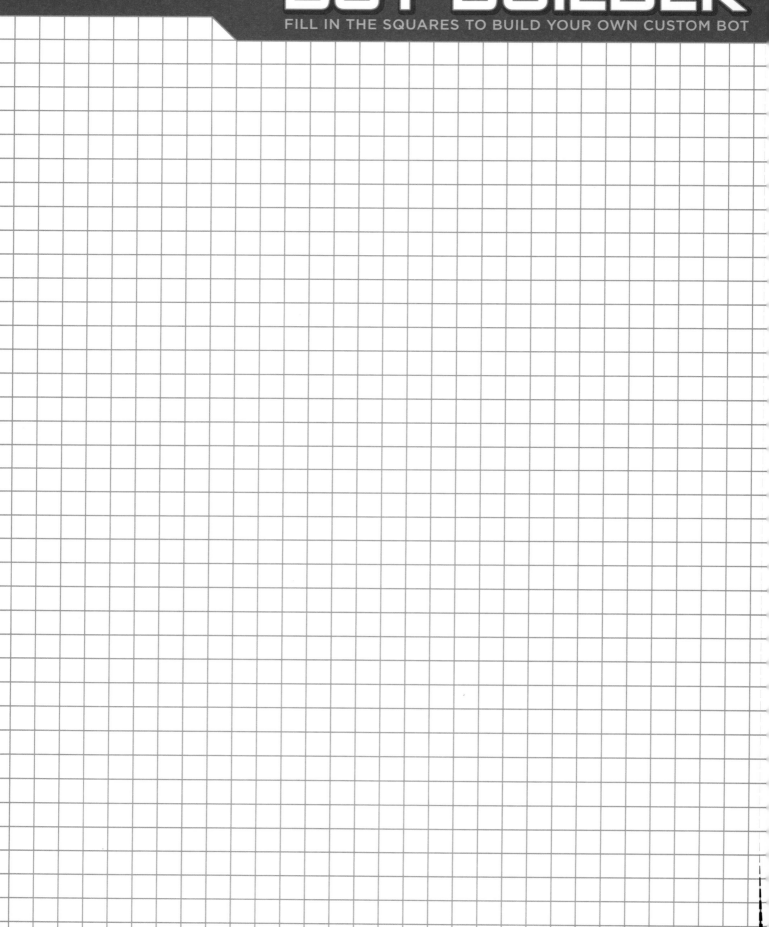

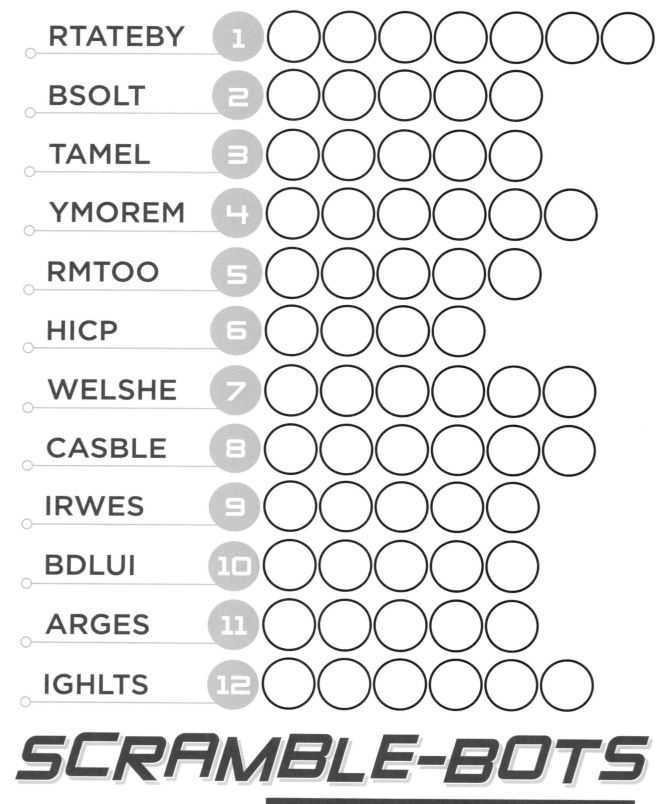

RTATEBY — 1 — ◯◯◯◯◯◯◯

BSOLT — 2 — ◯◯◯◯◯

TAMEL — 3 — ◯◯◯◯◯

YMOREM — 4 — ◯◯◯◯◯◯

RMTOO — 5 — ◯◯◯◯◯

HICP — 6 — ◯◯◯◯

WELSHE — 7 — ◯◯◯◯◯◯

CASBLE — 8 — ◯◯◯◯◯◯

IRWES — 9 — ◯◯◯◯◯

BDLUI — 10 — ◯◯◯◯◯

ARGES — 11 — ◯◯◯◯◯

IGHLTS — 12 — ◯◯◯◯◯◯

SCRAMBLE-BOTS

CAN YOU UNSCRAMBLE THE WORDS ABOVE TO SPELL OUT WORDS RELATED TO ROBOTS?

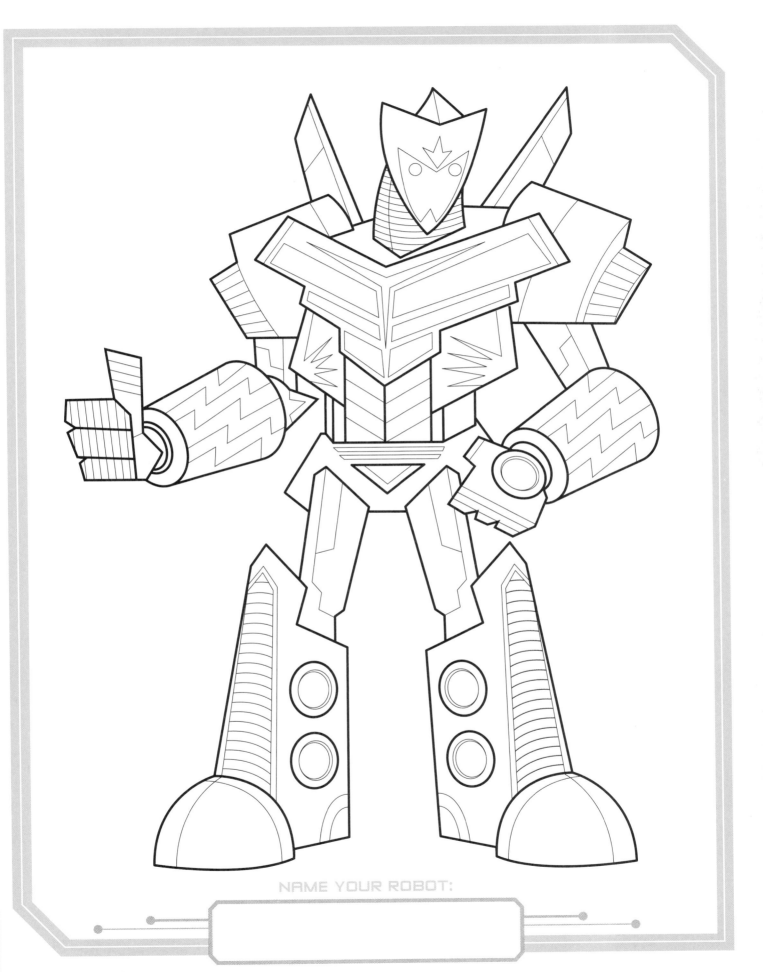

NAME YOUR ROBOT:

FACTOIDS & FUNNIES

■ A robot is a type of machine that can perform a set of actions automatically. Robots come in all shapes and sizes.

■ If a job is too dangerous for a human, a robot may be used to complete the task. Robots are used for things like handling hazardous chemicals and performing jobs in dangerous areas like volcanoes.

■ Robots have been sent to Mars to collect soil and rock samples. They analyze them and send the data back to Earth.

■ The history of robotics stretches back 2,400 years. The first robot was a steam-powered "pigeon," created around 400 to 350 BCE by the ancient Greek mathematician, Archytas, known as the father of engineering.

■ Virtual reality is a series of effects, made by a computer, that allows anyone wearing the special gear to feel like they are a part of an artificial world. Electronic gloves help the wearer "feel" the objects in the virtual world; a helmet produces the sounds and visuals.

FUNNIES

Q WHAT DOES A ROBOT FROG SAY?
A RIB-BOT!

Q WHAT DOES A ROBOT ADD TO ITS SALAD?
A VEGABOLTS!

Q WHY WAS THE ROBOT ANGRY?
A SOMEONE KEPT PUSHING HIS BUTTONS!

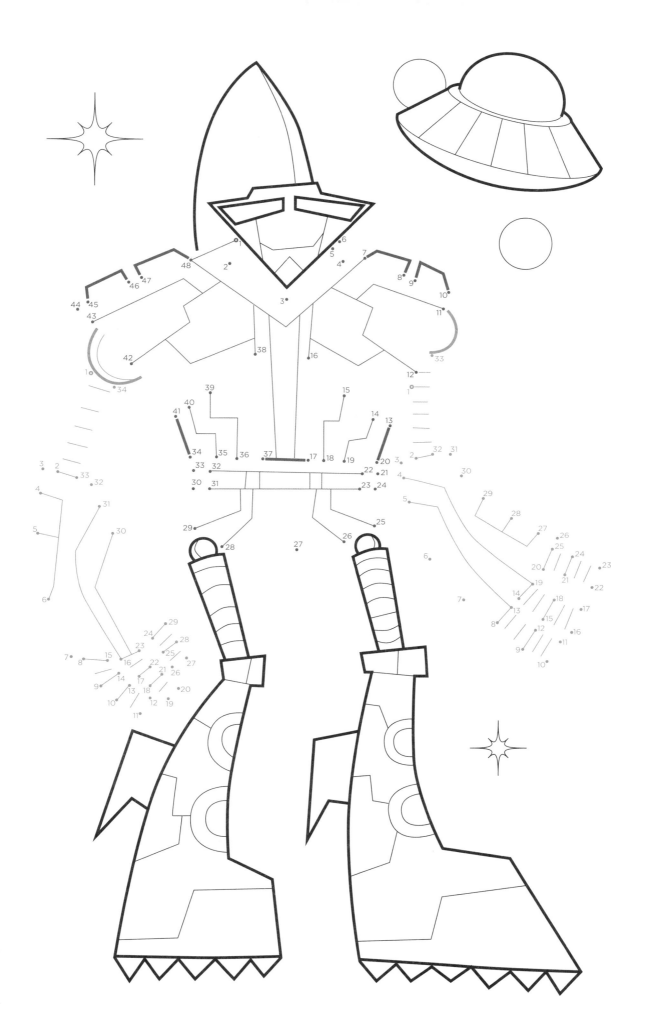

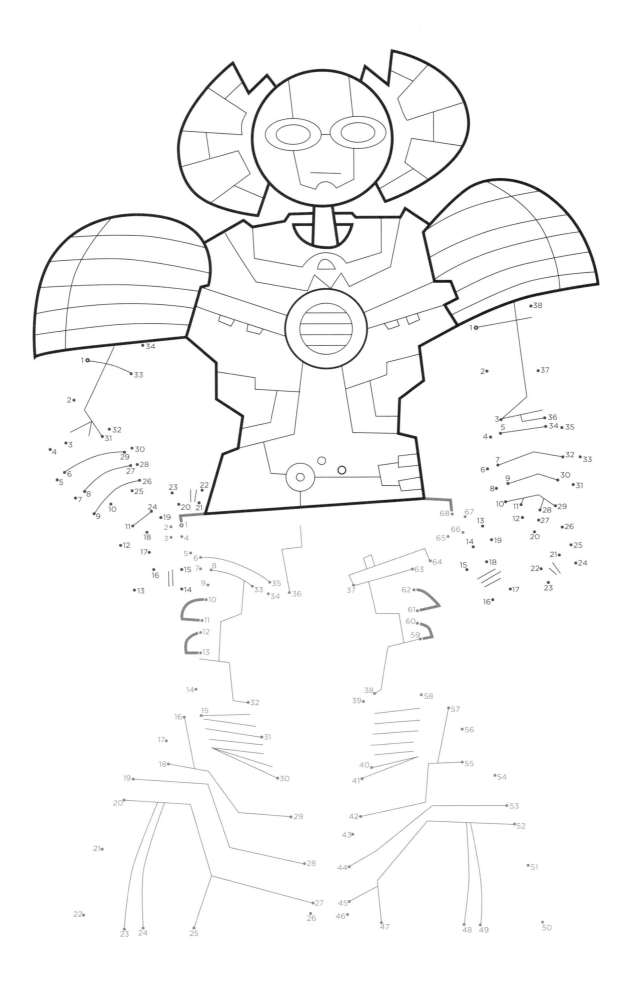

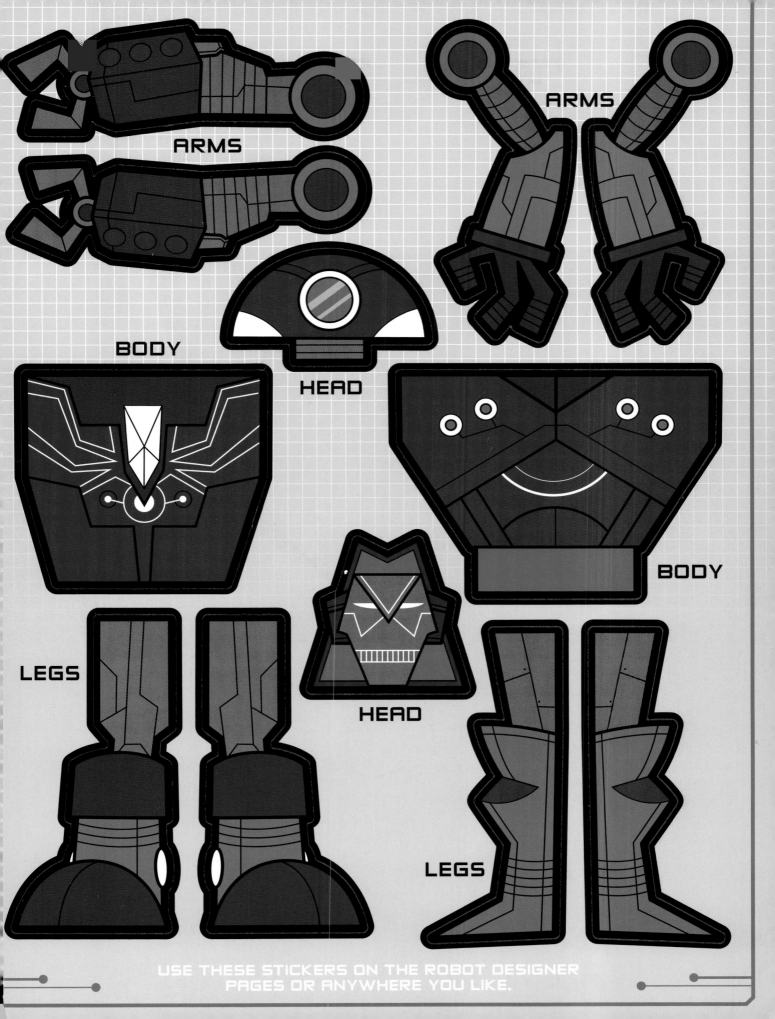

ARMS

ARMS

BODY

HEAD

BODY

LEGS

HEAD

LEGS

USE THESE STICKERS ON THE ROBOT DESIGNER
PAGES OR ANYWHERE YOU LIKE.